Radioactivity

Radioactive materials are generally associated with nuclear weapons, nuclear waste and accidents at nuclear reactors. We therefore tend to think of them as dangerous substances that must be avoided at all costs. It is true, of course, that many radioactive materials are very harmful, and if they are released into the environment, the results can be disastrous. However, we do derive many important benefits from the use of radioactive materials. Not only do they help to provide us with a considerable amount of electrical power, but they are also very important in modern medicine, industry and agriculture. And we can make use of the fact that we are surrounded by a number of harmless radioactive materials. In this book we look at the nature of radioactive materials, how they were discovered, what they are used for and how they affect the environment around us. The author, Mark Lambert, specializes in writing books for children on science and technology.

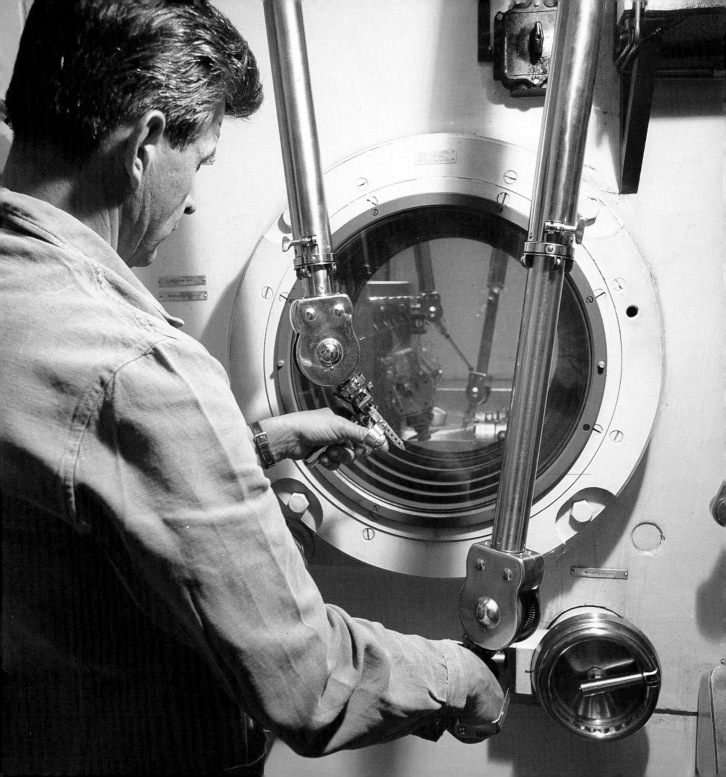

Focus on
RADIOACTIVITY

Mark Lambert

Focus on Resources series

Alternative Energy	Gas	Rubber
Aluminium	Glass	Salt
Building Materials	Gold	Seafood
Coal	Grain	Silk
Cocoa	Iron and Steel	Silver
Coffee	Meat	Soya
Copper	Nuclear Fuel	Sugar
Cotton	Oil	Tea
Dairy Produce	Paper	Timber
Diamonds	Plastics	Vegetables
Electricity	Radioactivity	Water
Fruit	Rice	Wool

Editor: Elizabeth Spiers

First published in 1989 by
Wayland (Publishers) Ltd
61 Western Road, Hove
East Sussex BN3 1JD, England

© Copyright 1989 Wayland (Publishers) Ltd

Phototypeset by Kalligraphics Ltd, Horley, Surrey
Printed in Italy by G. Canale C.S.p.A., Turin
Bound in the UK at the Bath Press, Avon

Cover *This patient's brain is being scanned using CAT (computer-aided tomography).*
Frontispiece *Handling a dangerous radioisotope by remote control in a hot cell.*

British Library Cataloguing in Publication Data
Lambert, Mark, *1946–*
    Focus on radioactivity.
    1. Radioactivity
    I. Title
    539.7′5

    ISBN 1–85210–432–5

Contents

1. Radioactive atoms

All matter is made up of tiny units called atoms. An atom is made up of a central nucleus surrounded by a cloud of particles called electrons. Each electron has a tiny negative electrical charge. The nucleus of the atom contains other particles — protons, which are positively charged, and neutrons, which carry no charge at all.

Not all atoms are the same. The numbers of neutrons and protons in the nucleus vary. This variation gives us the different elements of which everything around us is made. An element is a material whose atoms all contain the same number of protons and electrons. Examples include iron, oxygen, hydrogen and lead. Scientists know of over 100 different elements.

In most cases, the atoms are stable (not easily broken down) and do not change. However, some elements have unstable atoms that disintegrate, or decay (break down). They do this by

All three isotopes of hydrogen have one proton, but the number of neutrons varies.

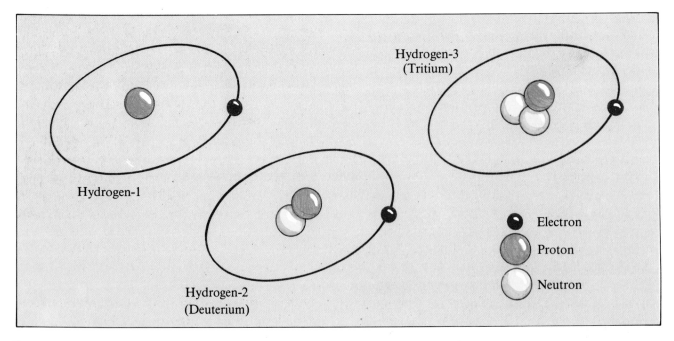

giving off radiation in the form of particles and high-energy rays. As they do this, they change into other elements. Uranium, thorium and radium are naturally-occurring elements that decay in this way. These elements are described as radioactive.

The type of element to which an atom belongs is shown by the number of protons in its nucleus; the number of neutrons affects only the mass of the atom (how heavy it is). It is possible to have two or more different forms of the same element, whose atoms have the same number of protons, but different numbers of neutrons. The different forms of the same element are called isotopes. For example, an atom of carbon normally contains six protons and six neutrons, but there is another isotope whose atoms contain six protons and eight neutrons. Isotopes are known by their mass numbers (the total number of protons and neutrons), so these two isotopes are called carbon-12 and carbon-14. Many isotopes exist in nature, and most of them are unimportant, but some, like carbon-14, are radioactive isotopes, or radioisotopes, and these are sometimes useful.

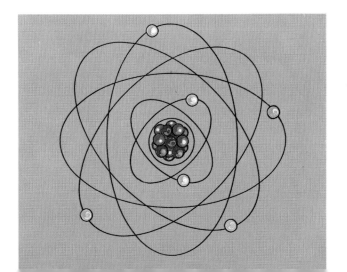

Above *Ernest Rutherford was the first person to work out the basic structure of the atom.*

Left *An atom consists of protons (blue), neutrons (red) and electrons (yellow).*

7

2. Radiation

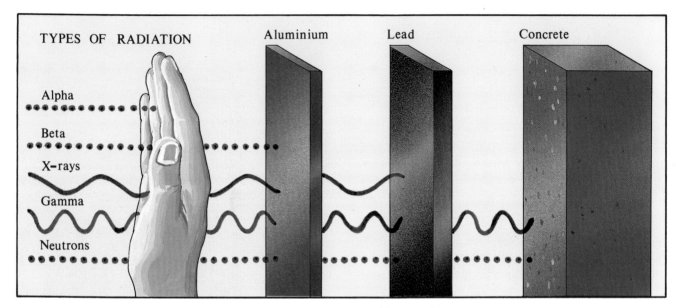

Radioactive materials emit (give out) radiation as they decay. There are several different types of radiation. Two of the most common ways in which radioactive elements decay are by emitting alpha or beta particles (also known as alpha and beta rays). Sometimes, a third form of radiation, known as gamma rays, may also be produced.

An alpha particle is made up of two neutrons and two protons. It carries a positive charge. Alpha particles are emitted at high speed, but they are easily absorbed (stopped), even by one or two sheets of paper. Alpha decay is fairly common. For example, the radioactive isotope

Different forms of radiation are stopped by different materials.

uranium-238 decays into thorium-234 in this way.

A beta particle is an electron moving at very high speed. In some radioactive elements, it is an ordinary negatively-charged electron, which is produced with a smaller, uncharged particle called an antineutrino. This happens when a neutron inside the nucleus of the atom changes into a proton. In other cases, a proton changes into a neutron, and the beta particle is a positively-charged electron, called a positron.

A cancerous growth has formed on the hand of this radiation victim from Hiroshima.

A neutrino is also produced. Beta particles are not as easily absorbed as alpha rays. Some can pass through more than 10 mm of wood, but can be stopped by a thin sheet of metal. Beta decay is very common. For example, thorium-234 decays into protactinium-234 in this way.

Protons and heavy atomic nuclei may also be emitted. Gamma rays are not particles. They are high-energy pulses of electromagnetic radiation – the type of radiation that includes radio waves, light rays, X-rays and cosmic rays. Sometimes, when the beta or alpha particle has gone from the nucleus, there is too much energy left behind. The nucleus throws out this energy in the form of gamma rays.

All these types of radiation affect living tissue, by breaking up atoms. However, gamma rays have the greatest penetrating power and cause the most damage.

A wax model of a young victim of the bomb dropped on Hiroshima.

3. The discovery of radioactivity

Radioactivity was first discovered in 1896 by a French scientist, Henri Becquerel. The year before, the German scientist Wilhelm Röntgen had discovered X-rays, and Becquerel was looking for new ways of producing them. He discovered that a substance containing uranium caused a photographic film to become fogged, and realized that uranium must be producing some kind of radiation. Several years later he discovered that the radiation carried a negative charge.

Marie Curie, a French chemist originally from Poland, then began to study this form of radiation, and it was she who first used the word 'radioactivity'. She discovered that there were three kinds of ray; positive, negative and uncharged. This was discovered at the same time by the British scientist Ernest Rutherford, who gave them the names alpha, beta and gamma rays.

Marie Curie went on to show that uranium was not the only radioactive element. In 1898, she showed that thorium was also radioactive. In the same year, she and her husband Pierre discovered polonium and radium. In 1902, they developed a method of preparing small amounts of pure radium from several tonnes of uranium ore. From her studies, Marie realized that atoms contain vast amounts of energy. In 1934, Marie Curie died of leukaemia, as a result of her exposure to radioactivity.

Henri Becquerel was the first to discover that certain materials produce radiation.

Marie and Pierre Curie in their laboratory in Paris in 1903.

Meanwhile, Rutherford and other scientists had shown that uranium and thorium break down into other elements as they give off radiation. A particular element breaks down at a steady rate, and Rutherford invented the term 'half-life' (see page 12) to describe this rate. Rutherford, and his assistant Hans Geiger, proved that an alpha particle is the same as a helium atom without its electrons. Rutherford died in 1934, believing that the energy contained in the atom could never be harnessed by humans. Two years later, nuclear fission (see page 20) was discovered by the German scientist Otto Hahn.

4. Measuring radioactivity

The atoms of a radioisotope do not all decay at once. At any time, only some of the atoms in a sample of such material are breaking down into new elements. Each different radioisotope has its own breakdown rate, called the half-life. This is the time that it takes for half the atoms in the sample to decay. During the next half-life period, half of the remaining atoms decay, and so on, until the last atom changes.

Half-lives vary considerably. Some are very short — the half-life of polonium-212 is less than a millionth of a second. Other radioisotopes have half-lives that vary from minutes to thousands of years. The half-life of uranium-238 is 4,510 million years, which means that just over half the world's uranium has decayed since the Earth was formed about 4,600 million years ago.

How quickly a sample decays is measured by counting the number of alpha or beta particles given off each second. The first counter was invented by the English scientist William Crookes in 1903. It had a screen coated with a substance that flashed every time it was hit by an alpha or beta ray. Ernest Rutherford and Hans Geiger used this type of counter, and Geiger went on to invent an instrument that records each particle as a click. Modern instruments count emitted particles electronically.

Rutherford and Geiger calculated that, in one gram of radium, 37,000 atoms would decay every second. The amount of any substance that

This diagram shows an element (blue atoms) with a half-life of ten minutes. After each ten-minute period, half the remaining atoms have decayed into atoms of another element (red atoms). This process continues until none of the blue atoms are left.

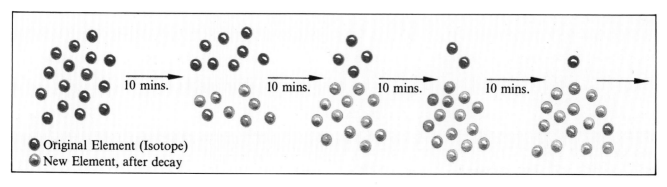

● Original Element (Isotope)
● New Element, after decay

will give the same number of disintegrations is known today as a curie. This is one of the ways that scientists use to measure radiation levels. Other units in use are the becquerel, rad (radiation absorbed dose), gray (a modern version of the rad), rem (roentgen equivalent man) and sievert. A fuller explanation of these units can be found in the glossary.

Using radiation counters to check evacuees, after the explosion of the Chernobyl nuclear reactor released a cloud of radioactive dust in 1986.

5. Uranium

Uranium is a hard, dense, whitish metal. It was first discovered in 1789 by a German chemist, Heinrich Klaproth. He named it after the planet Uranus, which had been discovered a few years previously. However, it was not until 1841 that a French chemist, Eugène-Melchior Péligot, managed to make a sample of the pure metal, and it was another 150 years before anyone discovered any real use for it.

Uranium is not a rare metal. In fact, it is more common in the earth's crust than several other elements, including gold, silver, mercury and iodine. It is radioactive, and can be found as three isotopes: uranium-238, uranium-235 and uranium-234. More than 99 per cent is uranium-238.

Uranium exists naturally in the form of several different ores, including uraninite,

A sample of pitchblende, a mineral commonly used as a source of uranium.

An open-cast uranium mine in Australia, where much of the world's uranium is mined.

pitchblende, coffinite and brannerite. Uranium ores are often found with those of other metals, and in South Africa uranium is a by-product of gold mining. The mining techniques used to extract uranium ore from the ground are much the same as those used for other mineral ores. However, in the case of uranium, how much ore there is, and where it is, can be found out by doing a radiometric survey.

The amount of radioactivity given out by a uranium ore is actually very low, so miners are not exposed to dangerous levels of radiation. However, uranium mines do have to be kept very well ventilated. This is to prevent the build-up of the radioactive gas radon, one of the products of the radioactive decay of uranium. Too much of this gas can cause miners to become overexposed to radiation.

15

6. Refining and using uranium

The rock that is mined from most uranium deposits actually contains very little uranium ore. Small amounts of ore are found in large areas of quartz. Each tonne of rock may contain less than 3 kg of uranium. The ore is extracted (separated from the rock) by mechanical processing followed by chemical treatment.

In the first stage of the extraction process, the rock is crushed, and sometimes sorted according to how radioactive the lumps are. These lumps are then ground up to a fine powder and mixed with water. This forms a thick, runny mixture called a slurry. The ore particles are harder and heavier than the quartz particles, so

Yellow cake is converted into nuclear fuel after a series of chemical processes.

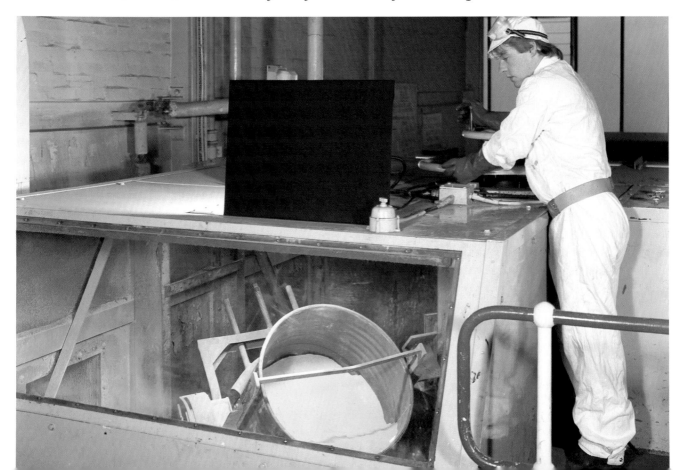

the pieces of ore fall to the bottom more easily. They can then be collected.

Chemical extraction begins with a process called leaching. Dilute acid (or alkali, in the case of some ores) is mixed with the ground up ore, and the mixture is heated under pressure while being stirred. Acid leaching produces a chemical compound of uranium that can be concentrated and purified. Further chemical treatment gives a material called yellow cake, which is about 60 per cent uranium. From this, it is possible to make a variety of uranium compounds, or uranium metal.

Uranium has only one use – as a fuel in nuclear reactors. However, this is very important; 1 kg of uranium can produce as much energy as over 2,700,000 kg of coal. It can be used in the form of the pure metal, in which case it is often alloyed (mixed) with other metals, such as aluminium, iron and molybdenum. Uranium compounds, such as uranium dioxide and uranium carbide, are also used as nuclear fuels.

Rotating kilns used in the production of metallic uranium fuel.

7. Elements in nature

A number of other radioactive elements occur in nature. Some of these are created when cosmic rays strike atoms of non-radioactive substances. This causes them to change into radioisotopes of another element. For example, a small amount of the nitrogen in the atmosphere is turned into carbon-14. Other natural radioisotopes include those of the elements zinc, antimony, mercury, tin, molybdenum and platinum. Even our own bodies have a little natural radioactivity – about 0.1 microcurie of potassium-40, which emits beta particles and gamma rays.

Many of the radioisotopes that occur naturally come from the decay of uranium or thorium. These elements begin four radioactive series, known as the uranium, actinium and thorium series. The uranium series begins with uranium-238. This decays into thorium-234, which in turn decays twelve more times, before finally becoming lead-206. This element is stable, and does not decay any further. Uranium-235 begins the actinium series, which ends with lead-207. It is named after the fourth member of the series. The thorium series begins with thorium-232 and ends with lead-208.

Natural radioactive materials form three series: the uranium (**left**)*, thorium* (**centre**) *and actinium series* (**right**)*.*

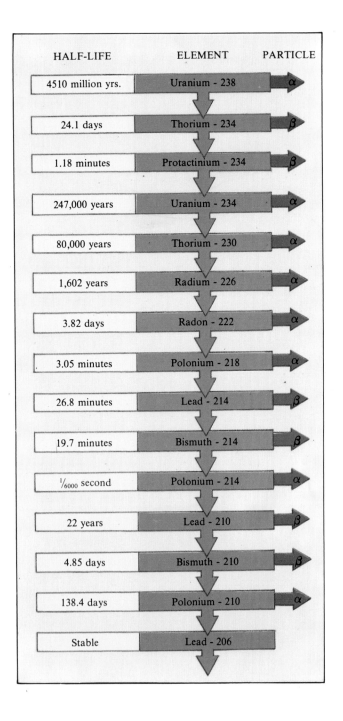

HALF-LIFE	ELEMENT	PARTICLE
4510 million yrs.	Uranium - 238	α
24.1 days	Thorium - 234	β
1.18 minutes	Protactinium - 234	β
247,000 years	Uranium - 234	α
80,000 years	Thorium - 230	α
1,602 years	Radium - 226	α
3.82 days	Radon - 222	α
3.05 minutes	Polonium - 218	α
26.8 minutes	Lead - 214	β
19.7 minutes	Bismuth - 214	β
$\frac{1}{6000}$ second	Polonium - 214	α
22 years	Lead - 210	β
4.85 days	Bismuth - 210	β
138.4 days	Polonium - 210	α
Stable	Lead - 206	

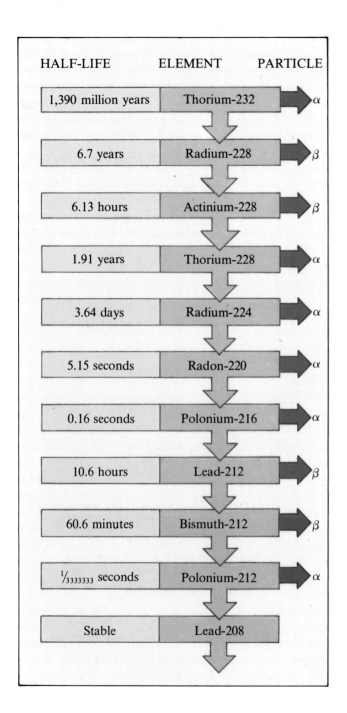

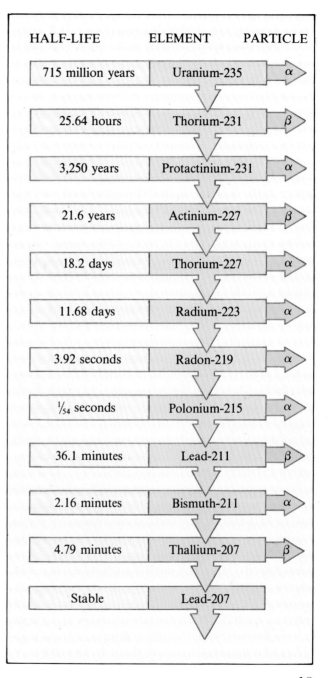

8. Fission and fusion

In 1938, the German scientist Otto Hahn, working with others, discovered that bombarding uranium with neutrons caused uranium atoms to split up, releasing a great deal of energy at the same time. Other scientists, in particular the American physicists Enrico Fermi and Leo Szilard, then suggested that the splitting process might produce more neutrons that could go on to split more uranium atoms. This would cause a chain reaction. The idea was soon proved correct. We now know that it is uranium-235 that splits. If enough uranium-235 is present − that is, more than the amount known as the 'critical mass' − the chain reaction keeps going. In an uncontrolled reaction, huge amounts of energy are suddenly released, causing a nuclear explosion.

In 1940, scientists discovered that atoms of another element could also be split. This was a new element, given the name plutonium. It was

Nuclear fission. When an atom of uranium absorbs a neutron, it immediately splits into two smaller atoms. At the same time, it gives out three neutrons (including the original one) and much energy.

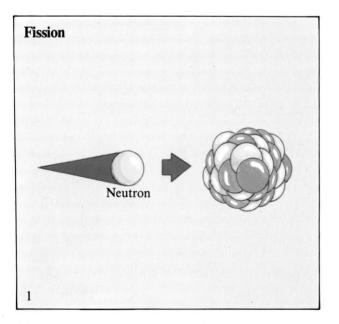

Fission

Neutron

1

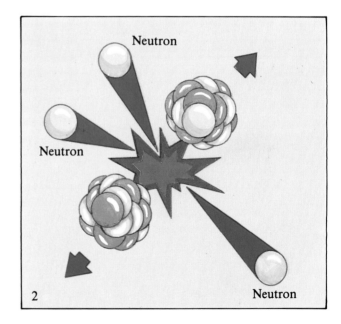

Neutron

Neutron

Neutron

2

one of the products of uranium fission. These materials were first used in weapons. On 6 August 1945, at the end of the Second World War, uranium was used in the atomic bomb dropped on Hiroshima in Japan. The bomb dropped on Nagasaki, three days later, contained plutonium.

Fission weapons of this type cause enormously destructive explosions, and make large quantities of radioactive dust, or 'fall-out'. One of the latest fission bombs is a battlefield weapon known as the neutron bomb. This is a smaller weapon that causes less blast damage and produces less fall-out. However, at the time of the explosion, it produces very strong radiation that is lethal to anyone nearby.

The most powerful nuclear weapons imitate the way in which the sun produces energy. This is known as thermonuclear fusion. In this process, the atoms of two isotopes of hydrogen, deuterium and tritium, are made to fuse (join together). They form atoms of helium, and vast amounts of energy are released at the same time. The fusion process produces very little fall-out. A thermonuclear warhead, however, is triggered by one or more fission explosions, which do produce fall-out. The warhead is also surrounded by a uranium casing, and in some cases this undergoes fission.

Nuclear fusion. Atoms of deuterium (one neutron and one proton) and tritium (two neutrons and one proton) are forced to join together to form helium. A neutron is also given out. In the process, vast amounts of energy are released.

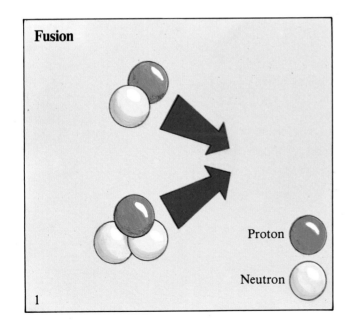

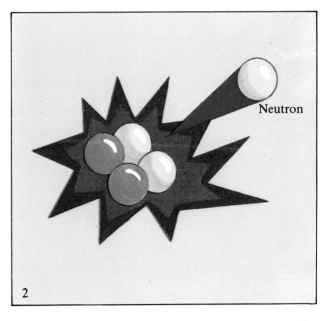

9. Power from the atom

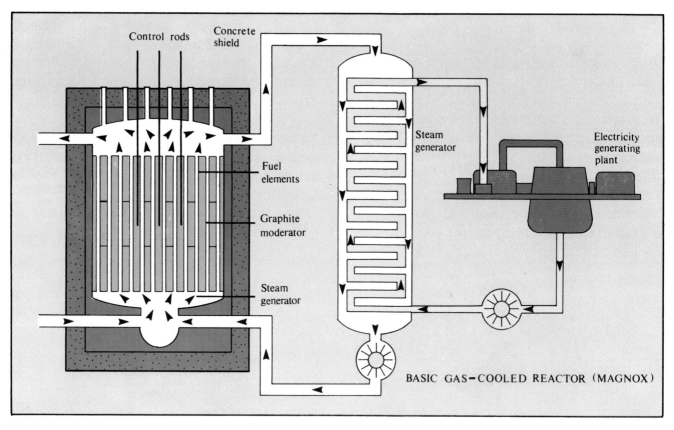

Control rods · Concrete shield · Fuel elements · Graphite moderator · Steam generator · Steam generator · Electricity generating plant

BASIC GAS–COOLED REACTOR (MAGNOX)

In a nuclear reactor, nuclear fission takes place in the fuel elements and the process is controlled by neutron-absorbing control rods.

Although nuclear fission can cause a devastating explosion, the process can be controlled to produce useful energy. This is done in a nuclear reactor, in which rods made of uranium or plutonium are used as fuel.

The fuel is contained in the core of the reactor. In order to slow down the chain reaction and prevent a nuclear explosion, the core also contains control rods made of a substance that absorbs neutrons, such as cadmium. The number of neutrons moving about the core can be controlled by raising and lowering these rods. This controls the reaction. The reactor can be shut down completely by lowering the rods into the core.

The reactor core also contains a material called a moderator (water or graphite), which slows down neutrons. This makes the reactor more efficient, as it is the slow neutrons that are more likely to split atoms of uranium or plutonium. High-speed neutrons tend to bounce off uranium atoms without causing any change.

Not all uranium is fissile (able to undergo fission). Over 99 percent of natural uranium is the non-fissile isotope uranium-238. Less than 1 per cent is fissile – the isotope uranium-235.

Natural uranium can be used as a fuel, but most reactors use a fuel that contains more uranium-235. This fuel is said to be enriched.

The uranium-238 is not useless, however. When atoms of uranium-238 absorb neutrons, they are turned into plutonium-239, which is a fissile material. This process is used in a fast-breeder reactor. A highly-enriched core of uranium and plutonium produces large numbers of neutrons. Some of these keep the nuclear reaction going, while others are absorbed by a blanket of uranium-238 around the core. Plutonium-239 forms in the blanket, and this type of reactor actually produces more fuel than it uses up, which is clearly a very economical process.

Rods of uranium metal fuel being inserted into Magnox cans.

10. Making new elements

Every element has one or more isotopes, many of which are radioisotopes. The gas radon, for example, has 17 different isotopes. Altogether, scientists know of about 1,000 radioisotopes. Many of these used to exist naturally, but have long since decayed into other elements. Today, only about 50 radioisotopes occur naturally.

The rest are all man-made, and scientists have even managed to create several completely artificial elements. Some of these elements and radioisotopes are formed by the process that goes on inside the fuel rods of nuclear reactors. Others are made by bombarding materials with high-speed subatomic particles in machines called accelerators, in which moving particles are speeded up by electric charges. Linear accelerators speed up particles along straight tubes, but the greatest particle speeds are reached using circular accelerators. One of the largest is the famous CERN synchrotron at Geneva in Switzerland, which has a 'track' over 6 km long.

A linear accelerator, used for producing intense bursts of neutrons.

The CERN synchrotron lies underground. The white circle indicates its location.

The element with the highest atomic number (the number of protons in the nucleus) that occurs naturally is uranium, with atomic number 92. Elements with atomic numbers of 93 or more are all man-made. As uranium is bombarded with slow-moving neutrons in a nuclear reactor, the elements neptunium (93) and plutonium (94) are created. Bombarding plutonium with neutrons produces americium (95). Curium (96) is made by bombarding plutonium with helium atoms in an accelerator. Californium (98) is made by bombarding curium with helium atoms. Elements with atomic numbers of up to 108 have been made, and in 1987, one group of scientists claimed to have created an element with an atomic number 110. These elements exist only briefly (element 110 is said to have a half-life of 9 milliseconds), but it is suggested that if super-heavy elements, with atomic numbers of 114 or more, can be created, they may be more stable.

25

11. Radioactivity in medicine

It is easy to detect radiation. If a radioactive material is present, it is possible to find out exactly where it is. This makes such materials useful as radioactive tracers, for following the movements of liquids or chemicals.

In medicine, radioactive tracers are used to help doctors to find any sign of disease inside the human body. For example, radioactive iodine is used to test how well the thyroid gland is working. The patient swallows some iodine

A gamma camera being used to locate a radioactive tracer in the patient's body.

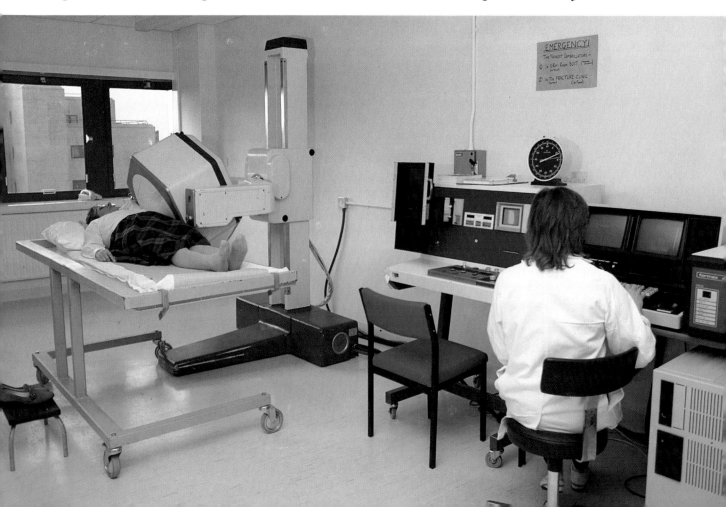

containing a tiny amount of the radioisotope iodine-131. It can be detected from the outside as it moves through the body. The amount that builds up in the thyroid gland shows whether it is underactive, overactive or working normally.

Various scanners and counting devices are used to locate radioisotopes in the human body. Modern scanners can find the exact position and size of any abnormal (unusual) tissue that might be there. This allows doctors to pinpoint areas of infection or cancer. One of the most advanced devices is the gamma camera, which can detect a source of gamma radiation. Gamma cameras are usually used to detect brain tumours. The radiation dose that the patient receives is often much lower than that of a normal X-ray.

A variety of radioisotopes are used as tracers. The hydrogen isotope tritium is used to help measure the water content of the body. Isotopes of potassium and sodium help in measuring the body's salt content. Strontium-85 is used to find bone tumours. Technetium, one of the products of uranium fission, is used to add a radioactive 'label' to a number of chemicals that are then injected into the body. These can be used to test how well parts of the body are working. The stomach, kidneys, spleen, liver, lungs, heart, brain and skeleton can be tested in this way. Scientists are now trying to discover a single chemical that can be used to detect tumours in any part of the body.

Gamma radiation is now widely used to sterilize medical equipment. It is thought to be quite safe to use. This method is particularly useful for sterilizing such things as rubber gloves, plastic blood donor kits and catgut thread, which are more difficult to sterilize using heat.

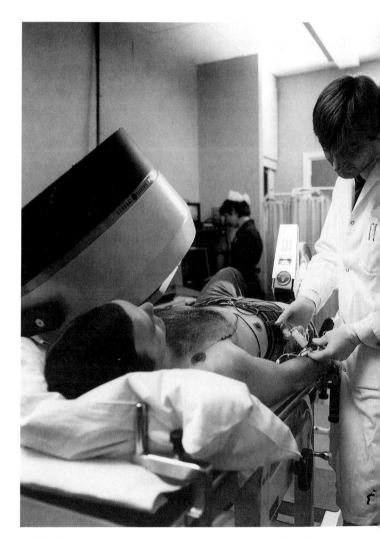

Injecting a radioisotope in order to check a patient's heart and lungs.

12. Radiotherapy

Large doses of radioactive materials kill living cells. These can be used to treat cancer by killing off the diseased cells. Some normal, healthy cells are killed in the process. However, cancer cells are killed by lower levels of radioactivity than normal cells. This is because cancer cells are dividing more quickly.

Radiation therapy, or radiotherapy, was once used for treating problems like acne and benign (not dangerous) tumours. However, the method uses radioactive materials which could be very dangerous, and could cause more dangerous cancers in the skin and other parts of the body. This is why doctors now use radiotherapy to treat only malignant (dangerous) cancers, and they make very careful calculations before starting treatment. The cancer is pinpointed exactly, using modern scanning machines linked to computers. These build up a three-dimensional (3-D) picture of the diseased part of the body.

Sometimes, treatment is given by injecting a radioisotope. This gives out beta particles inside the body. Cancer of the thyroid gland, for example, is treated by injecting iodine-131. This builds up in the thyroid gland, where the powerful beta radiation kills cancer cells, but does not do very much damage to nearby healthy cells. Radioactive phosphorus is used to treat leukaemia, bone tumours and several other diseases. A small tumour can sometimes be treated by putting a small piece or capsule of radioactive material into the body. Radium and radon are often used, as well as radioisotopes of caesium, cobalt, gold, iridium and tantalum.

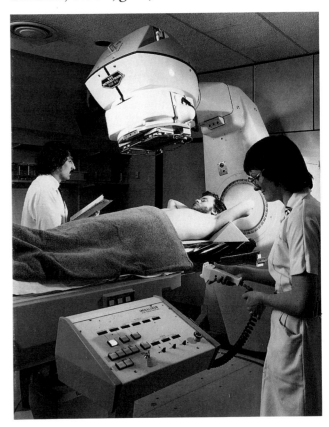

A radiation therapy machine containing 7000 curies of cobalt-60.

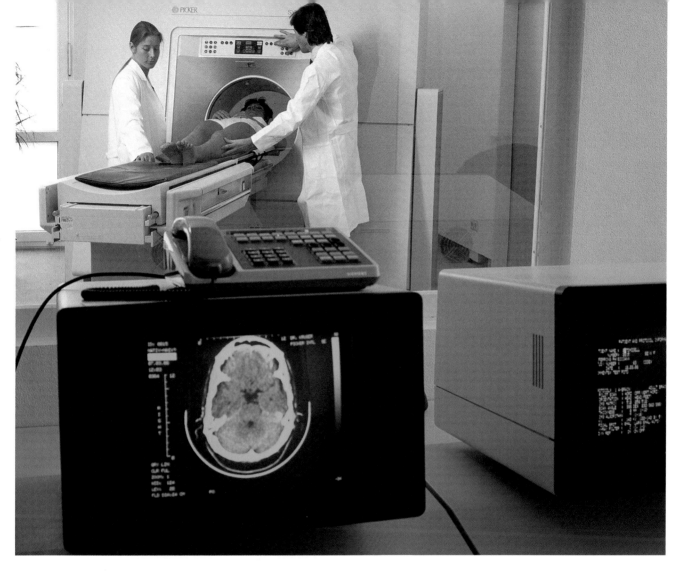

A CAT scanner can be used to locate the exact position of a brain tumour.

Cancers are often removed by surgery. To make sure that there is no cancer left, the patient may have radiotherapy from outside the body. This method is also used when surgery is impossible. A supervoltage X-ray machine delivers a powerful dose. The cobalt bomb machine uses cobalt-60 to produce a beam of gamma rays. Recently, scientists have discovered ways of using a linear accelerator or a cyclotron to treat tumours deep inside the body.

13. Radioactivity in industry

Radioactive materials have a number of industrial uses. Tracers can be used to find leaks in pipes. They are also used to follow the path of air pollution, and to study chemical processes.

Radioisotopes that emit gamma rays are used to examine metal castings, or welds in pipes. The rays pass through the material, and are picked up by a photographic plate on the other side. Any cracks or weak areas show up as darker spots on the plate, because more radiation can pass through.

Radiation is also commonly used to test the thickness of materials. A beta-emitting substance can be used to check the thickness of a sheet of material that is being shaped by rollers in a continuous process. The beta particles passing through the material are picked up by a detector. If the thickness varies, the number of particles that gets through also changes. The level of liquid in a sealed container, such as beer in a can, or liquid metal in a furnace, can be checked in a similar way.

A machine that uses beta radiation to measure the thickness of thin material.

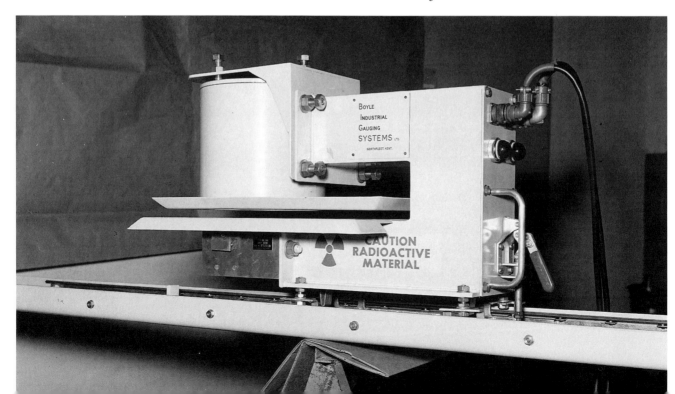

A radioactive material can also be used to check how quickly two surfaces that rub together are wearing out; for example, the piston rings that move up and down inside the combustion chamber of an engine. Some of the carbon in the piston ring is turned into carbon-14 by putting the ring in a strong beam of neutrons. When the ring is in place in the engine, and has been used for some time, the amount of carbon-14 in the engine oil can be checked.

A gamma-emitting radioisotope being used to check a welded joint in a pipeline.

If the level is high, the piston rings are wearing badly.

Sometimes very mildly radioactive materials are found in a few manufactured goods. Some modern compasses have luminous direction-finding marks that contain a tiny amount of tritium.

31

14. Radioactivity and agriculture

Radioactive tracers are often used to study plants and animals. By adding a small amount of a radioisotope to a chemical, a biologist can study how the chemical moves through a plant or animal. It shows where the chemical ends up, and how it is used. The radioisotopes usually used today are carbon-14, phosphorus-32, sulphur-35 and iodine-131. Among other things, they are used to study the effects of hormones and tranquillizers in animals, and insecticides and weed killers on crop plants.

Radiation affects the sex cells of animals and plants. It can make an organism sterile (unable to reproduce). This can be used to control some insect pests. Large numbers of a particular pest species are raised in a laboratory, sterilized by radiation and then released into the wild. There they mate with wild insects, but, because they are sterile, no offspring are hatched. This reduces the population.

Radiation of living cells may also cause mutations (changes) in a living organism's genes. Genes control the features of the organism, such as leaf shape, eye colour and height. Most mutations kill the offspring, but some may be

An image of the veins of a leaf produced by injecting the plant with the isotope potassium-42 and exposing a piece of photographic plate to the leaf.

useful. Many types of modern crop plant have been produced in this way.

Radiation can also be used to help preserve fruit, vegetables, meat, grain and other foods by killing off bacteria and insect pests. The radiation used is not strong enough to make the food radioactive. However, studies are still being carried out to make sure that it is completely safe and to find out whether the quality of the food is changed in any way.

A comparison of irradiated (**left**)*and untreated* (**right**) *strawberries.*

15. Handling radioactive materials

Radioactive materials are dangerous. A human who receives a radiation dose of more than 5 sieverts usually dies within 30 days. Lower doses can cause cancers that may take years to appear, so it is essential to make sure that those who work with radioactive materials receive as little radiation as possible.

Using a glove box to check small amounts of plutonium for impurities.

In Britain the maximum permitted dose (highest dose allowed) for an ordinary person is just 1 millisievert (one-thousandth of a sievert) over the whole body in one year.

A radiation worker is allowed a whole body dose of 50 millisieverts in a year, and there is also a 'professional emergency dose' of 250 millisieverts. A radiation worker may have this dose only once in a lifetime. This does not include any normal background radiation (see page 36), and recent evidence has suggested that the doses for radiation workers may be too high. The National Radiological Protection Board in Britain wants the maximum permitted dose in one year to be reduced to 15 millisieverts. In the USA, dose levels are controlled by the Environmental Protection Agency and the Nuclear Regulatory Commission.

To make sure that the dose is not too high, every radiation worker wears a small plastic dose monitor. This contains a small piece of photographic film. Some alpha-emitting materials can be handled in special cabinets fitted with built-in rubber gloves. More dangerous materials have to be handled by remote control in rooms known as caves, or hot cells. These are protected by concrete walls and thick glass. Areas where radioisotopes are handled are well ventilated, with filters that clean both the incoming and outgoing air. This prevents escape of radioactive materials. The rooms are built in a way that makes them fairly easy to decontaminate. When workers have to enter radioactive areas, they wear special protective clothing, which keeps radioactive dust off the skin.

In radioactive areas, workers wear protective clothes and carry radiation monitors.

16. Radioactivity around us

A radioisotope decays into another element, known as a daughter. If the new element is radioactive, it too will decay. This process continues until a stable daughter is formed. About 50 radioisotopes are found in the earth's crust; for example, radium and its daughters, members of the thorium series and potassium-40. They give off small amounts of radiation, known as background radiation. Tiny quantities of radioactive minerals are found in our drinking water. We also breathe in tiny amounts of carbon-14 and tritium, which are made in the Earth's atmosphere when cosmic rays or sub-atomic particles from outer space crash into particles of air.

Normally, background radiation is very low – less than 1.6 millisieverts per year, but some rocks and minerals contain more radioisotopes than others. There are a few places where radioactive minerals have collected near the surface. The monazite sands in the Kerala province of India are rich in thorium, and in places can give a dose of up to 28 millisieverts per year — well below the highest dose allowed.

Monazite sands often contain high levels of the radioactive element thorium.

Granite rocks at Land's End, England. They release radioactive radon gas.

Granite, like all igneous rocks, contains several radioactive materials. These are caused by the decay of radioisotopes present in the rock when it was formed. One of these isotopes is radon, a daughter element of radium. It is a gas, and therefore tends to seep out of the rock as it is made. Usually, this is blown away and causes no problems. However, it has recently been discovered that the gas can build up in people's homes. This means that homes in granite areas may have much higher levels of radioactivity than normal. The problem is known both in Europe and North America, and is particularly bad where homes have been built on the rubble taken from mines. Some homes have levels of radioactivity that are four times higher than the highest dose allowed for nuclear power workers. However, at the moment, air pollution is thought to be more dangerous to health than radon.

17. Radioactive dating

In 1988, radiocarbon dating was used to calculate the age of the Turin shroud.

Because radioisotopes decay into other elements until a stable daughter is formed (as explained in chapter 16), we can use natural radioisotopes to date (find out the age of) things that may be many millions of years old, such as rocks. If we know how quickly the stable daughter element is formed, we can work out the age of the rock, by measuring how much of the parent and daughter isotopes are present.

Different dating methods are used, depending on the type of rock (that is, the minerals it contains), and its age. The uranium-lead, thorium-lead and rubidium-strontium dating methods are all used to find out the ages of rocks over 10 million years old. The potassium-argon method can be used to date rocks formed as recently as 100,000 years ago. Volcanic rocks formed within the last 100,000 years are difficult to date using radioisotopes. However, the decay of lead-210 to bismuth-210 is used to date glacier ice, and sediments laid down in lakes and around coasts during the last hundred years. The decay of tritium into helium-3 can even be used to date old wines!

Carbon-14 is used to date materials made from once-living things. Carbon-14 is always being formed in the air, and living organisms take it in at the same time as normal carbon-12. They use it to build up body tissue. However, when an organism dies, it stops taking in

Glaciers can be dated from their content of iodine-129 or carbon-14.

carbon. The carbon-14 that is in the organism's body starts to decay into nitrogen. This happens steadily. Therefore, by measuring the amount of carbon-14 present in a sample of material, the scientist can find out its age. Carbon-14 is used to date wood, charcoal, cloth, shell, bone and sediments that contain organic (once-living) material. Carbon-14 has a half-life of 5,730 years, and the method is useful for dating materials from 50 to 500,000 years old.

18. Radioactivity and the environment

As far as we can tell, the natural radioactivity around us does little harm. However, we are increasing the amount of radioactive material present in the world, and many people are now concerned that we may be increasing the level of radioactivity in the environment to a dangerous point.

There are three main sources of man-made

In 1986, the Chernobyl reactor in the USSR was devastated by an explosion.

radiation. First, we produce large amounts of radioactive waste. Low-level waste, which comes from hospitals and research laboratories, is disposed of by encasing it in concrete and burying it in the ground, or dumping it in the sea. Medium-level waste from nuclear reactors and nuclear fuel reprocessing plants has also been dumped at sea. The high-level waste produced by the nuclear industry is stored under water in special tanks. However, the amount of this type of waste is increasing, and we will have to find some way of storing it safely for thousands of years. Special stores deep underground are being considered.

In theory at least, nuclear reactors are completely safe. Every effort is made to prevent the escape of radioactive material. However, there have been several accidents. The worst has been the explosion at the Chernobyl reactor in the USSR in 1986. Nuclear scientists believe that such an accident cannot happen again; others disagree.

Nuclear weapons are possible sources of lethal radiation. When weapons are tested in the open, fall-out may be carried thousands of miles. No one really knows what level of radiation is safe. Studies of the effects of radiation on humans have been going on ever since nuclear bombs were dropped on Hiroshima and Nagasaki in 1945. However, recent work has suggested that radiation levels that have until now been thought safe are not, in fact, safe at all.

Handling radioactive waste at the nuclear power station at Dounreay in Scotland.

19. Radioactive materials in the future

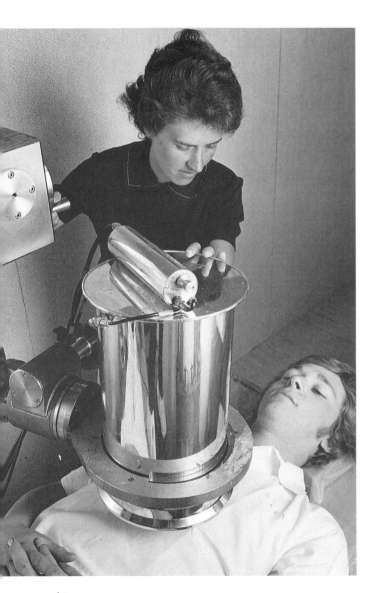

Radioactivity cannot be seen or smelt, but the effects of overexposure to radiation are horrifying. This is the reason why pollution of the environment by radioactive materials is greatly feared. They are among the world's most mistrusted substances. Most people link radiation with the most devastating weapons ever known, and we have yet to find a really safe way of dealing with radioactive waste.

On the other hand, radioactive materials are of great benefit. Uranium and plutonium provide us with a source of power that will last much longer than supplies of oil and coal. Critics of nuclear power say that, apart from the environmental dangers, the cost of the necessary safety measures makes it expensive. Industry and agriculture have benefited from the use of radioactive materials. Perhaps most important is that radioisotopes are vital in modern medicine, particularly in the diagnosis and treatment of cancer.

At present, there is considerable argument about whether the benefits of radioactive materials are greater than their disadvantages. Whatever the case, these substances already exist, and even if we wanted to stop using them, it is difficult to see how they could be banned

Plutonium-239 dust inhaled into the lungs gives out X-rays that can be detected.

In 1987, the two superpowers, the USA and USSR, agreed to begin reducing their stocks of nuclear weapons.

throughout the world. The number of nuclear weapons may be reduced for economic and political reasons, but it is unlikely that they will ever be banned completely. Also, it seems likely that nuclear fission will remain in use as a source of energy in the foreseeable future.

Facts and Figures

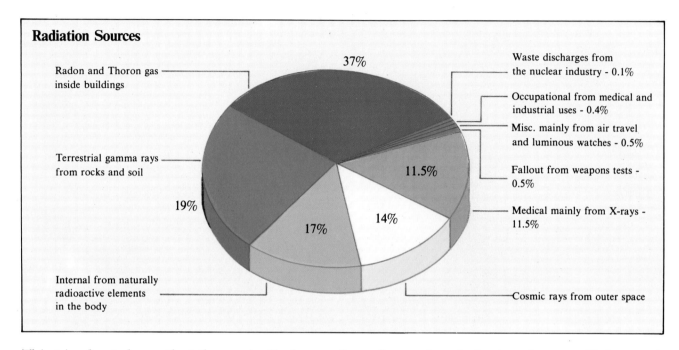

Radiation Sources

37%

Radon and Thoron gas inside buildings

Terrestrial gamma rays from rocks and soil

19%

17%

14%

11.5%

Internal from naturally radioactive elements in the body

Waste discharges from the nuclear industry - 0.1%

Occupational from medical and industrial uses - 0.4%

Misc. mainly from air travel and luminous watches - 0.5%

Fallout from weapons tests - 0.5%

Medical mainly from X-rays - 11.5%

Cosmic rays from outer space

This pie-chart shows that the waste discharges from the nuclear industry play very little part in polluting our world.

Glossary

Accelerator A device used to speed up charged atomic or subatomic particles, using magnets or electrical charges.

Alpha particle Particle emitted by radioactive material. Consists of two protons and two neutrons (the same as a helium nucleus).

Atom Smallest part of an element that can take part in a chemical reaction. It has a nucleus, containing protons and neutrons, surrounded by a cloud of electrons.

Becquerel The SI (Système Internationale) unit used to measure the radioactivity of an isotope. A material that decays at an average rate of one nuclear change per second has an activity of 1 becquerel. 37,000 million becquerels = 1 curie.

Beta particle A high-speed electron or positron emitted by a radioactive material when a neutron changes to a proton, or a proton changes to a neutron.

Cancer Harmful growth of living cells, which can spread through the body, often causing death.

Chain reaction *See fission.* Once started, the reaction proceeds without outside help.

Counter A device used to find the rate of decay in a radioactive material.

Cosmic rays Atomic nuclei and especially protons of very high energy that travel to earth from outer space.

Critical mass The smallest amount of a radioisotope needed to sustain a chain reaction.

Curie A unit used to measure radioactivity. 1 curie of a radioactive material is the amount that produces 37,000 million disintegrations per second. *See also* becquerel.

Cyclotron An accelerator in which the particles travel in an outwardly-moving spiral.

Decay The changing of a radioisotope into another isotope, by emitting alpha or beta particles.

Electron A very tiny, negatively-charged particle, which orbits the nucleus of an atom.

Element A substance whose atoms all have the same number of protons (atomic number).

Fall-out Radioactive dust that falls to the ground from the atmosphere after a nuclear explosion.

Fast-breeder reactor A nucleur reactor that uses little or no moderator, and makes more fuel than it uses up.

Fission Nuclear fission. A heavy atomic nucleus splits into two roughly equal parts. It can be caused when the atom is hit by a neutron (or other particle), or can happen naturally.

Fusion Nuclear fusion. Two light atomic nuclei join together to make a heavier nucleus. A large amount of energy is released at the same time.

Gamma rays Electromagnetic radiation of shorter wavelength than X-rays and longer wavelength than cosmic rays.

Geiger counter Geiger-Müller counter. Type of instrument used for detecting radiation.

Gray The SI unit used to measure the absorbed dose of radiation. It is the energy (measured in joules) absorbed by 1 kg of material. *See also* rad.

Half-life The time taken for half the atoms in a radioisotope to decay.

Hormone A chemical made by a gland. It travels through the blood, and affects other parts of the body.

Igneous rocks Rocks that were formed when lava became solid on or below the earth's surface.

Isotope Some elements have atoms that contain the same number of protons, but different numbers of neutrons. The different types of atom are isotopes of the same element.

Leukaemia A cancer-like disease of the blood, which affects the white blood cells. The causes of leukaemia are not known, but there seems to be a strong link between high exposure to radiation, and leukaemia. Radiotherapy is one of the treatments used.

Mass number The total number of protons and neutrons in a single atom of an element. Isotopes of the same element are generally known by their mass numbers.

Neutron An uncharged particle in the nucleus of an atom. Neutrons occur in all atoms except those of normal hydrogen (hydrogen-1).

Nucleus (plural: nuclei) The central part of an atom. It contains protons and neutrons.

Proton A positively-charged particle in the nucleus of an atom.

Rad A unit used to measure the absorbed dose of radiation. 1 rad = 1/100 gray.

Radiation Any rays or particles emitted from a source material. Examples are alpha particles, beta particles, neutrons, gamma rays, X-rays, cosmic rays, infrared (heat) rays and radio waves.

Radioactive A material whose atoms are unstable and decay naturally, giving off radiation. This can be alpha particles, beta particles and often, gamma rays.

Radioisotope A radioactive isotope.

Radiometric Involving the measurement of radiation.

Radiotherapy The use of radiation in the treatment of disease.

Rem (Roentgen equivalent man). A dose of radiation equivalent, in its effect upon living organisms, to 1 roentgen of X-rays.

Sievert The SI unit used to measure the dose absorbed by a living organism. 1 sievert = 100 rem. It is the same as 1 gray.

Subatomic particle Neutron, proton, electron, and a number of other small particles, all found in the atom.

Synchrotron An accelerator in which subatomic particles are made to travel along a circular tube, and can reach speeds near to the speed of light.

Tracer A radioactive substance used to follow the path of a chemical or a liquid. This may be in a plant or animal, a chemical reaction, or in a machine.

Tranquillizer A drug that calms you down.

Tumour A growth of living cells that serves no useful purpose in the body in which it has grown. A tumour may be benign (harmless), or it may be malignant, which is the same as a cancer.

Books to read

ASIMOV, I. *How We Found Out About Nuclear Power* (Longman, 1982)

BULL, A. *Marie Curie* (Hamilton, 1986)

DRISCOLL, V. *Focus on Nuclear Fuel* (Wayland, 1985)

HAWKES, N. *Nuclear Safety* (Franklin Watts, 1986)

JAMES, R. *The Super Powers* (Batsford, 1978)

KENT, A. and WARD, A. *Introduction to Physics* (Usborne, 1984)

MCKIE, R. *Nuclear Energy* (Macdonald, 1984)

MCCLORY, R. *Focus on Alternative Energy* (Wayland, 1985)

Sources of further information

For more information on the subjects covered in this book, please contact the following organizations:

Information Services
British Nuclear Fuels plc
Risley
Warrington WA3 6AS

Information Services Branch
United Kingdom Atomic Energy Authority
11 Charles II Street
London SW1Y 4QP

Office of Nuclear Technology and Safeguard
Bureau of Oceans, International, Environmental and Scientific Affairs
Department of State
Washington DC20520
USA

Atomic Energy Control Board
PO Box 1046
Ottawa
Ontario
Canada

Institute of Nuclear Sciences
Gracefield Road
Lower Hutt
New Zealand

Australian Atomic Energy Commission
Australian Nuclear Science and Technology Organisation
Lucas Heights Research Laboratories
New Illawarra Road
Menai
New South Wales 2234
Australia

Picture acknowledgements

The author and publishers would like to thank the following for allowing illustrations to be reproduced in this book: Amersham International, 31; British Food Research Association, 33; British Nuclear Fuels Plc, 15, 16, 17, 23, 34, 35; DMC Boyle, 30; CERN, 25; Geoscience Features, 14, 36, 37; St Mary's Medical School, 26; Topham Picture Library, 9, 11, 13, 38, 40, 43; United Kingdom Atomic Energy Authority, 24, 27, 28, 42; University of Liverpool Department of Botany, 32; Malcolm Walker, 6, 12, 18, 19, 20, 21, 44; Wayland Picture Library, 7, 8, 10, 22; ZEFA Picture Library, *cover, frontispiece*, 29, 39.

Index